BROKEN THINGS STILL BLOOM

Resilience from
a West Baltimore Childhood

BY CHANEL ROBINSON

Broken Things Still Bloom: Resilience from a West Baltimore Childhood
© 2025 Chanel Robinson

ISBN 979-8-98587336-8

Library of Congress Control Number: 2025939336

Printed in the United States of America

Dedication

For my children: In this life, you will face many challenges. Let my experiences teach you that no matter how bad things are in the moment, you can get through it and come out stronger on the other side.

For my best friend: Thank you for being my safe space.

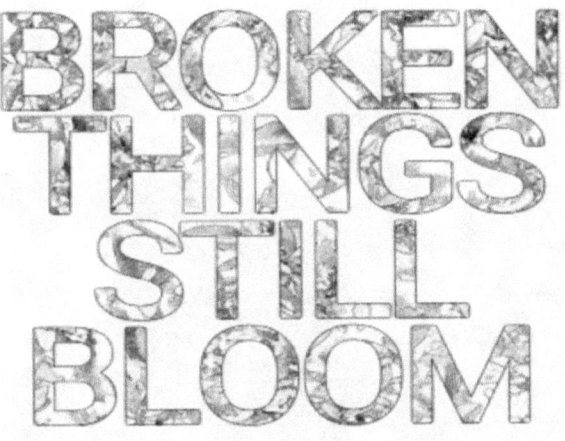

Table of Contents

The Strength I Didn't See

Two very important people in my life have told me, "You're one of the strongest women I know." I never thought of myself as strong. In my mind, I was just living, moving through life one day at a time. When situations came up, I did what was needed to get through them, and there were a lot of situations to get through.

Like everyone else in the world, I've had many life experiences. Some were good, some not so good. I've laughed a lot and cried a lot, but when the tears dried and a new day started, I moved on to the next thing. I didn't take the time I needed to work through my emotions; the thought never occurred to me.

Looking over my life and remembering different events, it amazes me that I didn't fall into some of the traps that ensnare or trip up others. They say people are a product of their environment. I watched people close to me live through drug addiction and abusive relationships. I was able to avoid physical abuse in my relationships, but I have been in emotionally abusive situations. One relationship in particular, I stayed in much longer than I should have.

The stories of my life have made it clear that my inner strength and the grace of God are the reasons I am still here.

Gilmor

Childhood is supposed to be about learning, growing, and having fun. It's about building relationships with family and friends and forming ideas about who and what you want to be. Growing up where I did and the way I did, I understood very quickly the big difference between fantasy and reality.

I lived in the Gilmor Homes Projects in West Baltimore City, a community of apartments set in red brick buildings. Depending on which court you lived on, you could be in a building with multiple units, or a court where the units resembled townhouses or rowhouses with two floors. I grew up in a townhouse.

I was raised in a home with a single mom, two younger brothers, and my mother's boyfriend. As a child, I wanted to become a teacher, a nurse, a lawyer, or a pediatrician. In an ideal world, my family would have a mom and dad who took care of our family and had lots of time to spend with us. That ideal was not the norm in Gilmor.

Most of the families in Gilmor lived in homes run by single moms. Some of the moms worked and some didn't. My mom worked jobs here and there, but never worked consistently. When she did work, it was mostly part-time; so, for much of my childhood, she was a stay-at-home mom. The kids in our neighborhood spent hours on the swings, playing dodgeball, hopscotch, or swimming at the public pool. My mom and her friends played cards with the music going or sat on the front steps, shooting the breeze.

In the projects during the '70s and '80s, it wasn't unusual to see drug deals happening. Some happened in my own house. It was normal to go outside and see guys, young and old, standing on the corners, hanging around, and talking. Some of them were dealing drugs, others were hanging out and flirting with the neighborhood girls. Some of the girls wanted to be with drug dealers because they had cars and money and would buy them things. The whole fantasy of the drug dealer girlfriend looked good in movies and on television, but in real life, it wasn't pretty.

One of my friends had a cousin named Dina who was involved with a drug dealer. Dina was friendly with my mom and hung out at our house sometimes. Her laugh was infectious, and she was always smiling. One night, Dina and her boyfriend were out when someone shot at his car. Dina was shot in the face and lost an eye. Her boyfriend was killed. She was devastated by her boyfriend's death and lived with the reminder of that night every time she looked in a mirror. I felt bad for her. She was a beautiful girl whose life was changed forever because she wanted to live in the fast lane.

The rationale for guys who were selling drugs was that they could make a few hundred dollars in one day, when others worked a

4

week to make just as much. They didn't seem to consider the downside of that kind of thinking. They didn't factor in the possibility of getting robbed, going to jail, or worse. All they cared about was fast money.

Ms. Ida was a friend of my mom who lost her son to gun violence. Ms. Ida lived down the street from us on Mountmor Court. We would see her coming home from work every day, and she would always speak to us. Sometimes she gave us a chance to earn a little change by getting her things from the corner store.

Her son, Leon, was tall and nice-looking. He wasn't what some would consider classically handsome, but he was easy on the eyes. Leon was about six feet tall, with chocolate brown skin and a crooked nose. He didn't lack for company. On many occasions, we saw him coming out of the house with a young lady heading out for the evening.

He was sitting on the steps of a house on Presbury Street when a fight broke out and someone started shooting. Leon was hit by a stray bullet and killed. He lost his life because he was in the wrong place at the wrong time. Leon was in his mid-twenties when he died. Ms. Ida's younger son died due to a health issue, and losing her older son to gun violence added to her pain. Not long after the shooting, she moved out of the neighborhood.

Some of the guys were in this life to "support their families", others were in it to support their drug habits. Most didn't think about the effect of their choices on their families. The ones who ended up in jail expected the women in their lives to "hold them down" by keeping money on their books and staying faithful until they came back home. My mother's boyfriend was a part of that life and spent some time in jail, which left her to care for three kids on her own. He was the father of my youngest brother, Tino. On Saturdays, she would go to the jail to visit him. She'd style her long, thick hair in curls, adding a touch of lipstick to complete the look. In the years before Tino was born, my mom left my brother and me with my grandmother when she went on these visits. Maybe she thought we were too young, or maybe she didn't want to expose us to a jailhouse environment.

During the week, he expected her to be at home to take his calls. I remember one time he called and asked, "Where's Angie?"

I said, "She's not here."

"Where did she go?"

"Out with Ms. Toni and Mr. Steve."

Then he said, "Tell her I called when she gets home."

He came home from jail a few months later. I woke up to the sounds of banging and crying in the room next to mine. He was cursing and calling her names.

Tears fell on my cheeks as I lay there listening to my mother being punished like a child. When I saw her the next morning, her face and arms were covered with red marks and bruises. As she sat on the sofa watching television, I hugged her and lay my head on her lap. I remember feeling guilty and thinking it was my fault for telling him she was out with her friends. He wanted to know who she was with, and one of the friends was a guy she'd known for years. Maybe he thought she was cheating on him, but he was wrong for hitting her.

Of my mother's two brothers, Uncle Ray was my favorite. He is only nine years older than I am, so he always felt like more of a big brother than an uncle. He was always looking out for us and got on us if we did something wrong. He cooked for us when my mom and grandmother were busy. I remember putting ketchup on my food one day and licking a drop that spilled onto the top of the bottle. Uncle Ray popped me on the mouth and said, "Don't do that, that's nasty!" I covered my mouth and looked at him with complete shock. That was the only time he ever hit me, and I never licked another ketchup bottle.

Uncle Ray was also a part of the street life back in the day. He was out one night wearing a white leather jacket he'd just bought when someone robbed him of his jacket and all of his money. He and some of his friends went after the guy, and they all shot at him. The guy was killed, and my Uncle Ray spent nine years in jail.

My grandmother never believed Uncle Ray was guilty. I remember her saying, "Ray wasn't the only one out there shooting. How do they know he was the one who killed that boy? It's not fair that he's the only one going to jail." She stood by him the entire time he was away, visiting him every Sunday after church. Sometimes my cousins and I were allowed to go with her.

My Uncle Irvin always drove us to the jail. He and my grandmother usually talked about the sermon of the day or where we would eat after the visit. We usually went to McDonald's or Horn and Horn Restaurant. My grandmother liked Horn and Horn because it was "all you could eat" for a low price.

Once we got to the jail, we waited in a big room full of chairs and vending machines. Uncle Ray would appear in the doorway of the visiting room, and Mama would greet him with a warm hug and a kiss on his cheek.

The visiting room was set up with benches, one facing the other. Mama always sat next to Uncle Ray.

She asked him, "How are you doing in here?" He always said he was okay. I don't think he would have told her if anything was wrong. He wouldn't want her to worry more than she already did.

Uncle Ray checked in with us. He would say, "Hey, baby girl. How's school going? Are you keeping up with your homework?"

I was 14 when he went away, and I missed having him around. I wrote to him, so he knew I was thinking about him. I liked to draw and color pictures as a kid. I would send him my artwork so he'd have something pleasant to look at. The only image I had of what a prison cell might look like came from movies and cop shows. They portrayed it as a small space with a twin-sized bed, dull gray walls, and a steel door with a small window in the middle. When he wrote back, he always asked for more pictures. Drawing was very relaxing for me. I still color sometimes as a way to de-stress.

Uncle Ray got out of jail in 1991, just a few months after my second child was born. He got his barber's license and started working in a shop. When my oldest son was about twelve, Uncle Ray let him work in the barber shop, sweeping up hair and running to the store for the other barbers so he could earn a few dollars on the weekends. It made my son feel good to come home and show me how much money he made. Uncle Ray became an example of a man who made a mistake, took responsibility, and then made a good life for himself.

My Uncle Ray and Dina are just two examples of what can happen when you make certain choices in life. Dina made a choice to be with a boyfriend who was in the street life and that increased the chance of violence might follow him. Uncle Ray was able to move forward and become a role model for the young men in our family.

Life in the projects wasn't all bad. I enjoyed playing outside with kids in my neighborhood. My best friend was a girl named Valerie. We met when we were in the same third-grade class, and her family lived down the street from us on Mountmor Court. Valerie was the youngest of six sisters, and sometimes my mom let me spend the night at their house.

When Valerie and I were little, her mom would fix her hair in ponytails with colorful rubber bands. My hair would be in ponytails one week and braids the next. It was a special occasion when our

9

moms let us wear our hair out in curls. This usually happened for Easter or on school picture day.

Valerie became my friend when we realized we lived on the same court. I was sitting on my front stoop, and she came by and said, "Hey Nelly." She was the only person I let call me that. "Do you wanna come down to my house and play jacks?" she asked.

"Sure," I said. After that, we played together almost every day.

I had another friend named Lisa whose grandmother owned the neighborhood corner store. Ms. Anderson's small store sold canned goods, bread, milk, lunch meat, snack items, and sodas. It was a place to get little odds and ends to carry us over until we did our big grocery store shopping. A lot of families in the projects received public assistance and food stamps, so there were times when money was low. When my mother got her food stamps for the month, we were able to go to the supermarket and stock up on what we needed.

Ms. Anderson was the kind of person who enjoyed helping her neighbors. She allowed people to get items on credit if they didn't have money to pay. Sometimes my mother sent me to the store, and Ms. Anderson would write in her book the items we bought and how much we owed. My mother always went to the store when she received her check from the state on the first of the month to settle her account.

I spent hours with Lisa and Valerie jumping rope, romping on the playground, and playing jacks on the front steps. Valerie always declared, "I'm the oldest, so y'all have to do what I say."

There was one problem with her claim: we were all born in the same month, just days apart. I was always reminding Valerie that we were all the same age, and she was only two weeks older than me. She had a very strong personality, so we let her have her way most of the time. I've never been a confrontational person, and it didn't seem worth arguing with her over something so minor. If there was something I really didn't want to do, I could always leave and go home.

We met our friend Janice in middle school after her family moved onto the court. Janice was fun. She lived with her mom and three older sisters. We hung out at their house playing cards and watching movies. Janice was a big fan of scary movies like Carrie and Friday the 13th. I hate scary movies, so I spent a lot of time covering my eyes, and they had fun teasing me.

I remember watching *The Exorcist* and *Rosemary's Baby*. But it was another movie that truly haunted me. I can't remember the name, but a witch sneaks into a little girl's room and cuts off her ear while she sleeps. For years after seeing that movie, I went to sleep with my hand over my ear so no one could come in the middle of the night and cut it off. From that point on, I was done with scary movies.

The Women Who Raised Me

When I was very young, we lived on Booker Court just a few doors down from my grandmother, whom we all called Mama. In our family, it was normal for us to call our grandmother Mama and call our mothers by their first name. I wonder if it was because my mother and aunts were all teenage mothers. My mom had me at 16, and my Aunt Marsha gave birth to her first daughter at 15. Most of the women in my family became mothers as teens. I was 20 when my first child was born, 11 days after my birthday. My Aunt Tammy became a mom at 19, and she's the only one whose children never called her by her first name.

My grandmother was a woman of faith who loved her family. When I was younger, she spent time with friends playing cards, having drinks, and listening to music. On Saturday afternoons, she went to thrift stores with her sister-in-law, looking for bargains. They usually came home with used toys for the kids, knick-knacks for the house, and sometimes a few items of clothing that she thought we needed.

My grandmother was a single mom of five who cleaned houses for white families who lived outside of the city. She let me go to work with her one day, and we took the number 21 bus downtown, then caught a commuter bus to Columbia, a big suburban planned city in a nearby county. The ride from Baltimore to Columbia takes about 30 minutes by car. Since we were traveling by bus, the ride was closer to an hour.

When we got to where she worked, I was impressed by the large houses and manicured lawns. In the projects, there was a small patch of grass between the houses. The Afro-American newspaper used to hold an annual "Clean Block" contest, and all the neighbors came together to plant flowers and paint their front doors, anything to make the court look pretty. One year, someone painted a hopscotch board in the middle of the court, and we spent hours jumping around and playing on it. I can't remember if Gilmor Homes ever won the contest, but it was heartwarming to see everyone come together to make the neighborhood look good.

The houses in Columbia were big, single-family homes. They were separated from one another by large green lawns. Some had swimming pools and attached garages. Inside were two-story foyers, wall-to-wall carpet, and chandeliers hanging from the ceiling. In the projects, you walked through the door and up a flight of stairs to get to a living room and kitchen with concrete floors.

The family Mama worked for referred to her as "Miss Hilda" instead of calling her by her first name. To me, this meant even though she worked for them, they showed her respect.

We walked into the house and were greeted by the mom; I don't remember her name. "Good morning, Ms. Hilda."

She looked at me with a smile and asked, "Who is this?"

"This is my granddaughter, Chanel."

"Hi Chanel, how are you today?"

In a quiet voice, I said, "Fine."

She shook my hand and said, "Nice to meet you." After giving Mama instructions on what needed to be done in the house, the mom left for work.

I spent the day watching her go from room to room, cleaning and washing, making everything in the home tidy. When I watched her clean the inside of the refrigerator, I noticed how different their food was from ours. The staple items were the same, like milk, eggs, and butter, but they had cheese and fruit I'd never seen before, like bleu cheese, blueberries, and kiwi. I was used to apples, oranges, bananas, and sliced cheese with plastic wrapping.

Mama worked a lot, and as the oldest child, my mom was responsible for looking after her siblings. The relationship between my mother and grandmother became strained once my mom became a teenager. According to Uncle Ray, my mother was very headstrong and wanted things her way. She didn't want to listen to Mama. She became the typical teen who thought she knew what was best and no one could tell her anything different.

At the age of 14, my mother met a man who was 21. Mama was against the relationship because of the age difference. I'm sure she thought what a lot of people probably thought: a 21-year-old man only wants a 14-year-old girl for one thing, sex. Because my mom was so much younger, I think it was easy for him to mold her into someone he could control. According to Uncle Ray, my mother and grandmother fought a lot because Mama was trying to stop my mom from seeing this man. The harder Mama pushed, the more defiant my mother became. She would run away and spend days at a time with this person. There came a point where Mama didn't know what to do with my mom, so she sent her away.

My mother had a teacher she trusted. Her name was Ms. Coleman, and she offered to let my mom stay with her for a while; Mama agreed. The idea was, since my mom seemed to respect Ms. Coleman, she might listen to her about this relationship not being in her best interest. I don't know how long she stayed with Ms. Coleman, but eventually, she went back home and hatched a new plan that involved the young man who would become my father. My mother knew that my father liked her and that Mama really liked him. She started seeing him and eventually became pregnant with me. My great-grandmother was a minister, and she believed that if you created a child with someone, you should marry.

My parents married four months after I was born. My father enlisted in the Army and was able to provide housing for his new family. My mother, now in a new apartment in the projects, was free to do whatever she wanted, and Mama couldn't stop her. She ended up back with her old boyfriend while my father was away. Once my dad came home and saw that my mom had moved her boyfriend into the apartment, he ended their relationship. Hearing this story gave me a better understanding of my mother as a young girl. She got caught up with an older man whose influence on her was so great that she was willing to go against her mother's rules to be with him.

During our elementary school years, we spent a lot of time at my great-grandmother's house. I remember spending summers at her place on Riggs Avenue with my brother Brian and my cousins, Dana and Towanda.

My great-grandmother lived in a row home with white marble steps. In Baltimore, row homes with marble steps were a sign of middle-class achievement and a source of pride. Every Saturday, my great-grandmother and other ladies in the neighborhood took a bucket of water and a can of Comet or Ajax and scrubbed their front steps. It was a good time for neighbors to come together and chat about the events of the day while making the block look fresh and clean. Sometimes she would let us girls clean the steps.

Reverend Clara Ann "Tinnie" Chaney, or Grandmama, as we all called her, was a minister who kept us in church. She was an associate pastor at the Gillis Memorial Christian Community Church– the first woman in Baltimore City to be appointed to that position. Every Sunday, we sat close to the front so she could keep an eye on us from the pulpit. Anytime one of us fell asleep during the service, she signaled one of the ladies in the pew to nudge us awake. She was intent on teaching us about the bible and how important it was to live a life according to God's teachings.

Every Saturday afternoon, she hosted bible study classes for the neighborhood kids. I think some of them came for the crackers and juice she gave us afterward. I believe she felt it was her job to teach young people the importance of knowing God and living by faith.

Grandmama lived next to Mr. Sampson's Luncheonette. Mr. Sampson's was a neighborhood staple. It was a small place, not enough room for tables, just a counter, some stools, and a kitchen area behind the counter where you could watch the cooks make your food. It was a hole-in-the-wall type of place, and it was always crowded. Everyone knew Mr. Sampson made a great fried pork chop sandwich. Grandmama would get herself a pork chop sandwich on white bread with mayonnaise and hot sauce.

We loved it when she bought us french fries from Mr. Sampson's. He would dump the fries into a brown paper bag straight out of the fryer and sprinkle them with salt and pepper. She would put some fries on each of our plates with a hot dog or hamburger that she made. We covered the fries with ketchup, and they tasted so good. She would give us forks, but we preferred to pick them up with our fingers. They were warm and soft, and when we licked our fingers, we could taste the combination of ketchup, grease, and salt. You could hear a chorus of *mmm's* from everyone at the table. Sometimes there were little crunchy pieces at the bottom of the bag. Those were my favorite, and they still are today. It was always a treat to see Grandmama come into the house with that greasy bag of fries.

17

Grandmama was one of the sweetest ladies I ever knew, but she didn't play when it came to keeping us kids in line. She was a disciplinarian when necessary. She was definitely a "spare the rod, spoil the child" type of person. That's why I did my best to stay out of trouble. She was very strict when it came to things like lying; that was a major sin in her eyes. If one of us got in trouble, which was usually my cousin Dana, you might be sent out to the backyard to get a switch off the bush or she would swat you on the butt with her hand.

You couldn't say certain things around her. If one of us said something like, "I'm gonna kick your tail," she would correct us and say, "People don't have tails, only animals have tails." We also couldn't say the word *butt*. She referred to it as your behind or hind parts.

My cousin Towanda used to suck on her fingers as a child. Grandmama would threaten to put hot peppers on her fingers to get her to stop. I don't know if she ever followed through with her threat since Towanda sucked her fingers until she was a teenager.

Grandmama spent a lot of time playing the piano and teaching us hymns. She had a black upright piano that stood against the living room wall. A few times, she let me sit next to her on the bench and play as she showed me the different keys. Grandmama didn't listen to secular music and didn't allow it to be played in her house. She would pray with us before we went to bed and kiss us all on the forehead before saying goodnight.

Grandmama passed away when I was ten years old. One of

my favorite memories of her was combing her hair. She had the prettiest silver-gray hair, and she would let me comb it for her every day. Back then, a lot of ladies straightened their hair with a hot comb that they put on the stove. Her hot comb had metal teeth at the end of a long black wooden handle. You had to be very careful when using the hot comb on the little hairs at the nape of your neck. It was easy to get burned if you moved while getting your hair done. Her hair felt so soft. It made me feel like a big girl because she trusted me to comb her hair and grease her scalp and make her look pretty. Grandmama wasn't an overly affectionate person, but we always knew she loved us.

Ties That Bind

My childhood was more bitter than sweet. I was the quiet one who always stayed in the background, not wanting to be the center of attention; a skinny little girl who was teased for wearing thrift store clothes.

My brother Brian and I liked to play a game we made up where we had imaginary spouses and children. We were the closest in age, so most of my time was spent playing with him. We spent hours in our little world with the families we created, living life as we thought it should be.

In our early childhood, we shared a room and had bunk beds. We used our sheets to create a fort on the bottom bunk and turned it into an imaginary car for our "families". At night, when we were supposed to be going to sleep, we would watch TV and laugh. We spent many afternoons watching *Batman*, *Speed Racer*, and *The Flintstones*.

My mother sent us to the laundromat on Saturdays to do the family's wash. Some days, if she didn't feel like cooking or if there wasn't much food in the house, she would give us money she got from her drug dealer boyfriend and send us to the Chinese food place to buy dinner. Brian and I were not happy about taking that walk, especially if it was late.

"Man, this really gets on my nerves," I would say. "I don't know why he couldn't get the food before he came into the house."

"I know, it's not like he won't be eating too," said Brian. "He could've just stopped on the way in."

"They act like we don't have to get up for school tomorrow. Why are we having to go out at 9 o'clock at night to buy food?"

"Because they're too lazy to do it."

When our cousins came over, we played school or church. Brian was the preacher, mimicking the sermon we heard in church on Sunday. My cousins and I were the choir, singing songs like *In the Garden* and *Jesus Loves Me*. When we played school, I was the teacher because I was the oldest. We used a small chalkboard where I wrote words and math problems for us to solve. It was good practice.

When I was about 12, I learned how to braid, and sometimes my aunt Marsha asked me to braid my cousins' hair. I liked doing their hair, and there were a few times that my aunt gave me a couple of dollars for my work. I really enjoyed that part. There were many Saturday afternoons when we sat on the front stoop surrounded by friends, talking and laughing while one at a time I would do Dana and Towanda's hair. After both girls' hair was braided, we all went to the playground to sit on the swings and watch the neighborhood boys play baseball.

Sometimes Aunt Marsha let me spend the night at her house. It was good to be with the girls without my brothers around. We'd sit up when we were supposed to be going to sleep and talk about boys, which ones we thought were cute and which ones weren't. My aunt didn't let Dana and Towanda spend the night at our house. She didn't trust my mother's boyfriend.

My brother Tino was five years younger and had developmental delays; what they used to refer to as *retarded* back in the day. My mother said he was sick with meningitis as a baby. It affected his intellectual development, but you could only tell if you were talking with him. He had to speak slowly so people could understand what he was saying. He would go through spells where, if he was frustrated or upset, he would hit his head on the floor or the wall. We spent a lot of time trying to stop him from hurting himself. Tino loved music. Any time my mom played records or turned on the radio, he would drop to the floor and rock back and forth.

Everyone in the neighborhood knew Tino and understood his situation. Sometimes he would walk into their houses without knocking. When he liked someone, he sat next to them on the floor and rubbed their legs. He never meant any harm, he just liked being around people.

When we were younger, he spent most of the time with my mom. When we got a little older, my mom let him go outside to play, and it was my job to keep an eye on him. I would get annoyed when I wanted to do something with my friends but couldn't because I had to watch him. If I tried to take him with me, he whined because he didn't want to go, which annoyed my friends. My friend Valerie used to say, "Why can't you just leave him? He'll be okay."

I worried that if something happened to him, I would be blamed. My mother trusted me to look out for him, so if he made too much of a fuss, I wouldn't go.

A part of me resented my mother because I felt she was pushing the responsibility of taking care of her child onto me. *Why did I have to be the one to watch over him? Why did I have to go through the embarrassment of not being able to do what I wanted with my friends because he didn't want to go with us?* These were things I said to myself every time I had to stay behind and deal with him instead of doing what I wanted to do.

One of my favorite memories of my early childhood is of my mother. I loved sitting on the living room floor with her, singing along to the records she played. She loved Gladys Knight and the Pips, Stevie Wonder, and Earth, Wind, and Fire. Her favorite was Diana Ross and the Supremes. I loved singing with my mother; to me, she sounded just like Diana.

My mother's name was Angela, and just like Diana, she was a

23

slender woman with long, thick, and beautiful brown hair. She loved to sing and even entered a talent contest when she was a teenager. I think I got my love of music from her. She listened to a variety of artists. She enjoyed groups like Fleetwood Mac, Steely Dan, and The Beatles. My brother teased me when I was a teenager because I liked Bon Jovi and Duran Duran. He would jokingly call me a white girl because I would listen to rock and pop instead of hip-hop. Like my mom, I didn't choose music based on black or white. I liked whatever sounded good to me.

Innocence Lost

In the beginning, Angie was a great mom. She would get us up for school, cook meals for us, and take us to visit family. When she made fried fish and potatoes, she would make a small portion without onions just for me because she knew I didn't like them. Her staple meals included oatmeal for breakfast and bologna and cheese sandwiches for lunch. As a treat, we might get Cream of Wheat instead of oatmeal. At some point, there was a shift, and she became a different type of mom. She wasn't as hands-on as she had been. She slept in almost every day. More and more often, Tino would get himself up, dressed, and run out to meet his school bus.

I can't pinpoint exactly when it happened, but I was about 9 years old. My mother wasn't at home, and I'm not sure where she was. What he asked me to do seemed strange. *Why did he want me to do that? Why was he showing this to me?*

"Just kiss it," he said. "It won't be so bad."

It just felt wrong, and I really didn't want to do it, but I also didn't want to make him mad. I thought if I just kiss it quick, like a peck on the cheek, that would be it, but it wasn't. He wanted more than just kissing it. It was nasty and gross, and I just wanted it to be over. He made me promise not to tell anyone, especially my mother. He said if I did, he would beat me, and she wouldn't believe me anyway. I'd seen the way he treated my mother. I had no reason to think he wouldn't follow through on his threat. I was scared and confused. I didn't understand what was happening or why.

He started waking me up at night when everyone was asleep. When it was done, he always gave me a dollar. I guess that was supposed to make me feel better; it didn't. It was like I was being paid for a service, a job I never applied for. After each time, I would get back in bed and go to sleep like nothing ever happened. I tried to put it out of my mind until the next time I was woken up in the middle of the night. I spent a lot of time trying to be happy, but I couldn't escape the anxiety of not knowing if I'd get to sleep through the night.

His name was Marvin. He was the father of my youngest brother. He entered my mother's life when she was 14 and he was 21. I guess, liking young girls came to him early in life. In fact, every time he cheated on my mother, it was always with someone much younger. I don't remember him ever having a job, unless you count selling drugs as a job. He went to jail a few times because he sold drugs. I guess it was during one of those times that my parents got together.

My father's name was Jimmy. He wasn't around much when we were growing up. He came to get Brian and me a few times a year, usually for a holiday or when it was time to shop for school clothes.

My parents were 16 and 17 years old when I was born. They got married not long after I was born, and Brian came along the following year. My parents were married for such a short time, I don't remember them living together. The story I was told was that they planned to get pregnant and marry so my mother could move out on her own. The plan worked.

My father was in the Army and spent time in Vietnam. From a very young age, I only remember my mother living with Marvin. Marvin was one of those guys you'd see on the corner hanging around and selling drugs. He was very abusive to my mother. I woke up many nights to the sound of him cursing and hitting her. Other nights, when I would hear her saying "no" over and over, then a few minutes later I would hear the squeaking of the bed springs because she gave in and let him have his way. Whenever I heard these sounds, I put my pillow over my head and tried to think of something that would drown them out.

The two of them sat around on the first of the month, waiting for the mail to come. He always went with her to the liquor store where she would cash her welfare check. I'm sure he got a portion of it as soon as she got the cash in her hand. I used to wonder why she put up with him for as long as she did.

I didn't understand the dynamics of an abusive relationship until I was older. I think their seven year age difference and her inexperience at the time they met made it easy for him to manipulate and control her.

One time, Marvin and I were in the kitchen, and my mom was asleep upstairs. My body had started to change. I was getting breasts, and my butt was getting a little rounder. I didn't look so much like a little girl anymore. I was being chastised for something; I think maybe I forgot to wash the dishes or clean the kitchen. He held a belt in his hand and had me pull my pants down as if he was going to spank me like when I was little, only he just stood there looking at me.

Neither of us heard my mother come down the stairs, and we were surprised when she walked into the kitchen and saw me standing there. She asked what was going on, and he said he was about to beat me. I remember her saying, "She's too big for that." He got mad and went upstairs.

When she followed him upstairs, I could hear them arguing. A few minutes later, he came down and went out the door. It was clear to me he was upset that he was interrupted, but I was glad she came down when she did. I hate to think of how far he may have gone if she hadn't.

28

She never said anything to me about what happened, we just went on with the rest of the day. Looking back, I wonder what went through her mind that day. Did she suspect something might be going on? If she did, would she confront him about it? I've made peace with the fact that some questions will never be answered.

I looked forward to the weekends I stayed at my grandmother's house. It gave me a chance to get away from the anxiety and worry about whether I'd get to sleep through the night or not. Mama loved to play music while she cleaned house on Saturday mornings. Her favorite was Al Green. If we didn't wake up to *Let's Stay Together* or *Love and Happiness*, it would be gospel music by Shirley Caesar or Andre Crouch. I felt safe at my grandmother's house. I used to ask if I could live with her, but my mom always said no.

During the week, I liked being at school; I especially liked my fifth-grade teacher, Mrs. Koeger. I discovered at an early age that I liked to write. I didn't feel comfortable verbalizing my thoughts and feelings, but writing was a good way for me to express myself. Mrs. Koeger was a heavy-set woman with graying, curly hair. She was very encouraging and gave one-on-one time to anyone who needed extra help.

One day, she mentioned that her cat had kittens, and I told her, "I wish I could have one." A few weeks later, she came into the classroom holding a big paper bag. She handed the bag to me, and I opened it to find the cutest white kitten. I named her Tessa after a character from a TV show I used to watch. I was so nervous about taking her home. I wasn't sure my mom would let me keep Tessa, but she did. I loved playing with her and waking up to find her at the foot of my bed.

It seemed like every time Tessa got out of the house, she would end up with a new litter of kittens. I think the final straw was her using my mother's plants as a litter box. After a few times cleaning cat poop out of her plants, Mom said Tessa had to go. It broke my heart.

When I was about 12 years old, I came to a point where I couldn't keep the secret anymore. *But how do I tell my mother? Would she believe me? Would she be mad at me? Would it finally stop?* I had to get this out. Fear kept me from telling. I couldn't face her reaction, but I had to get this out.

I decided to do what I did best; I wrote a letter. I wrote down everything I needed to say. I wrote the truth about everything he made me do. I was afraid to give it to her, afraid of her reaction, afraid of what would happen next. *How would he react? Of course, he would deny it. Would he come after me? The situation might get worse.* All I could think was, I'm not ready to face it all right now. I told myself, *maybe I'll give it to her later.* I put the letter in a drawer and didn't think about it anymore.

One day, my mom got my brothers and me together and we went to my grandmother's house. As we walked the short distance, she was kind of quiet. As soon as we went into the house, my mom went straight upstairs to my grandmother's room. I didn't think too much about it, but then I heard my name being called. I got to the bottom of the stairs and looked up to see my grandmother with a piece of paper in her hand. My heart sank to my stomach. I met her at the top of the stairs and saw my mother sitting on the bed. She was crying.

My grandmother looked me in my eyes and with the letter in her hand, she asked me, "Is this true?"

I looked at her, then at my mother, and said, "Yes."

It broke my heart to see how much this information hurt my mother. She held onto me and cried. I felt a sense of relief that she wasn't upset with me. I worried that she would blame me or take his side. I thought maybe things would change and finally get better. I'd be able to go to bed and not worry about anything happening.

We didn't go home that night. My grandmother called the police, then the real circus started. Police interviews, followed by a visit to the emergency room. The one part of this crazy situation that made me feel good was he would finally be out of the house. I would finally be free of him, or so I thought.

He was arrested and eventually charged with sexual abuse of a child. Going through that trial was one of the hardest experiences of my life. I was only allowed in the courtroom when it was my turn to testify. I think this was because I was a minor. It seemed like his eyes never left my face the entire time I was on the witness stand. I could feel him staring at me, and I was more nervous than ever before. There was a woman on the jury with whom I made eye contact. Of course, I didn't know her, but the way she looked at me gave me comfort. With each question I answered, I kept my eyes on her. I told my story directly to her. I remember my mother being in the room, but I didn't look at her. I felt more comfortable focusing on a stranger's face.

When the trial was over, he was acquitted. I'm not sure what went wrong. Did they not believe me? Was it some sort of technicality? This was never explained to me. What bothered and surprised me the most was that a few weeks later, he was back in the house. When I look back at it now, I realize the situation was so unfair. There was no conversation or explanation, he was just back. It was as if nothing ever happened. At this point, I was 13 and was forced to live with this monster, and I had no say in the decision. My mother allowing this person back into our space was like a slap in my face.

How could she let him back in? Did she not believe me? What was the point of going through all of this? I never asked her any of these questions. I didn't think any of her answers would satisfy me. I'm not sure what I expected her to say. How could she possibly explain this?

We were taught early on to never question the decisions of

adults. On the one hand, we were told it was okay to speak our minds, but if we said anything the adults didn't like, we would get in trouble. You could get popped in the mouth or be put on punishment for "being disrespectful." Soon after moving back in, he started coming to my room again. I didn't tell anyone when the abuse started again. I didn't see the point. I became a person who kept my emotions inside. I avoided conflict because I was always worried about the other person's reaction. I started staying out of the house as much as possible, hanging out with friends, spending time with my cousins, or spending the weekends at my grandmother's house. When I was in the house, I kept to myself. I stayed in my room listening to music, reading, or writing. I wrote poetry. I drew pictures and colored them—anything to stay out of the way.

One night when he came to get me out of bed, I decided I wasn't getting up. I don't know what made me so defiant, but I refused to move. No matter how many times he said to get up and come downstairs, I just lay there staring at him, not saying a word. He stood in the doorway with this look of confusion and disbelief, but I didn't care. He wasn't going to get his way this time. After a few minutes, he gave up and went downstairs. I slept well that night, but I didn't try that again.

Once he asked me what I would say if anyone asked me about what was going on. Without stopping to think, I said, "I don't know because I hate your guts."

He slapped me across the face, hard. When I started to cry, he hugged me and said he was sorry. He asked, "So, you really hate me?" I shook my head without a word. I had seen him hit my mother like that and knew that from then on, I had to watch what I said to him.

When I was 15, I met a guy from the neighborhood who was 19. His name was Daryl. He was a part of a group of guys who rode through the block every Friday night on their bikes. My friends and I used to sit on the steps of a vacant house, talking, laughing, and people-watching. We were mainly boy-watching like teenage girls do. One night, they stopped and started talking to us. I'm not sure what it was about Daryl that made me want to talk to him. He wasn't what you would call handsome, but he wasn't ugly either. He was funny, though, and I like a guy who can make me laugh. After spending a little time with him, I decided I was ready to officially lose my virginity, and he was going to be the one to get it.

Since the age of 9, I was forced to do sexual things that I did not want to do, but this was going to be my decision. The experience wasn't a good one, and once Daryl got what he wanted, he moved on to the next girl. Giving myself to this guy didn't have the effect that I thought it would. I don't know what I thought was going to happen. Maybe I thought I would get a little of my power back since I was doing it because I wanted to and not because I was being forced.

Looking back on it, I didn't know him very well, and it wasn't a serious relationship. Still, when he moved to the next girl, my feelings were hurt. It was as if I didn't mean anything to him; not that I should have, since, as I said, we didn't know each other very well. I was completely in my feelings about what I perceived as rejection by a guy I hardly knew, all the while my nightmare at home was still going on.

The way it ended was just as strange to me as the way it started. I don't know if he sensed that something was different about me, but he seemed to know that I wasn't a virgin anymore. I think once I got to a certain age, he may have been afraid I would get pregnant, so he never penetrated me.

The day this saga ended, I believe my mother was at work. He talked with me, and he asked, "Do you want all of this to stop?"

I didn't say anything. I just stared at him, not sure where this conversation was going.

Then he said, "You know if you want this to stop, all you have to do is say so."

I remember thinking, *Is that it? Can it really be that easy?* He asked me again if I wanted it to stop.

Finally, I said, "Yes."

Then he told me, "All you have to say is I don't want you to do this anymore."

I looked at him and said, "I don't want you to do this to me anymore."

He looked at me for a minute, then walked away. And just like

35

that, it was over. He never bothered me again. A part of me wondered if I said that to him earlier, would it have stopped then? But then I thought, no; he stopped it when he wanted to stop it. It didn't matter what I wanted, he had control of the situation the entire time.

Biding My Time

The next three years, I spent each day longing for the day I could leave home. My mother became someone I didn't like or want to be around. She was addicted to drugs and wasn't the mother we needed her to be. She smoked marijuana and drank wine with her friends when we were younger, but she'd moved up to the harder stuff. Once Brian and I became teenagers, things started to shift. There were a lot of people in and out of the house. When we went outside, she locked the screen door so we couldn't get back in unless someone came to unlock it. She didn't want us walking in on something we shouldn't see.

One day, I walked into the kitchen when she, Marvin, and some of their friends were sitting around the table. I saw some white powder on a mirror on the kitchen table. That was the day I discovered Marvin was selling drugs out of our house. I resented my mother because she allowed my abuser to come back into the house.

And because of her addiction, I was left to care for their son. I didn't understand how she could be with someone who would do such a horrible thing to her child. She was supposed to protect me. I was so angry because I felt like she was putting Marvin ahead of me.

Watching her interact with him as if everything was normal, I felt she had abandoned her responsibility to me as a parent.

I needed to keep myself distracted, so I stayed out of the house as much as possible and hung out with my friends. We used to sit on the wall in front of Janice's house. Sometimes we'd go to the corner liquor store and buy snacks, and Valerie and Janice would buy beer. Back then, they weren't checking IDs like they should have been, so it was easy for them to get what they wanted. I tried beer once and didn't like the taste. I would get root beer instead. Hires was my favorite because of its creamy taste.

Some of the girls smoked weed, which I also tried. I didn't smoke it, I let Valerie give me a shotgun—once. She held one end of the joint in her mouth and blew the smoke into mine. I didn't like that either and never tried smoking it. I wasn't good at inhaling, and I never wanted to risk going home and having my mother smell marijuana on me.

In high school, I had a different group of friends. I hung out with Tammy, Marie, and Stacy, aka Pete. I met Tammy and Marie in middle school, and we became close. We had a lot of classes together, and most of the time, the same lunch period. Stacy was the only guy in our little group. He was smart and funny and always kept us laughing. Like other high schools, you had cheerleaders and the girls who wore designer jeans like Jordache and Gloria Vanderbilt. One girl owned Levi's jeans in every color. It was normal to see girls with Michael Jackson t-shirts and buttons.

It seemed like 1983 was Michael's year. Everywhere you looked, his face was on a shirt, a button, a notebook, or a magazine cover. I even had a Michael Jackson sequined glove. My bedroom wall was covered with photos of Michael, New Edition, Tevin Campbell, and Babyface.

In the spring of 1982, I went to Daryl's house to visit his sister Debbie. We became friends when I started hanging out with her brother. We were watching television when a friend of Daryl's came into the house. He was a little over six feet tall, with caramel brown skin, and was very handsome. He didn't say very much, he just stood in the middle of the room. His name was Marcus, and I thought he was the cutest boy I had ever seen. He was part of Daryl's bike club, but I didn't remember seeing him when the guys rode their bikes past me and my friends on Friday nights.

I'm not sure how it happened, but after a while, Marcus and I started talking, and eventually, I started going to his house to hang out with him and his friends on his front porch. Marcus lived with his mom and his grandparents. I had crushes on guys before, but Marcus was different. He was the first boy who showed an interest in getting to know me, and not just because he wanted to get into my pants.

Most of the time when I was around him, I didn't say a lot. I just liked being in his presence. Being with him gave me a chance to escape the madness that was going on at my house. Whenever his friends went home and we were left alone, he would sneak me into the basement of his house so we could make out until it was time for

39

me to go home. He was the best kisser. He had soft, full lips. The kisses started out slow and intensified the more we got into it. He liked to stroke my hair with one hand and rub my back with the other. When we were in that moment, it was like no one else existed.

There were times when he'd go off on his bike with Daryl and leave me to wait. I sat on his front porch for hours. His mom or grandmother came to the door periodically to find me still sitting and waiting. His mother thought I was crazy, but waiting for him was better than going home.

One of the best times I spent with Marcus was when he deejayed my 16th birthday party. I spent most of the night ignoring my friends. I stayed in the corner with him while he played records. I remember dancing with one boy, but I couldn't take my eyes off Marcus. We just kept looking at each other while I was dancing with someone else. We didn't dance together once. He stayed in the corner and played the music, and I was happy he was there.

When it was time to go to my junior prom, there was no one I wanted to go with but him. I asked him to go with me, but he said no. He was going to his senior prom around the same time with another girl. I was so disappointed; I decided I wasn't going.

My mother didn't want me to miss out on what she thought would be a great high school experience. She asked the son of one of her friends if he would take me to the prom, and he agreed. His name was Lamont. He was about nine years older than I was. I had been around him many times, and he seemed like a good guy. I knew he agreed just to be polite, and since it seemed so important to her, I changed my mind about going.

I started to get excited about prom night. My mom bought me a long white dress with wide sleeves that almost looked like angel wings when I held my arms out on each side. Most of the other girls wore short dresses, which I was told was more appropriate for a junior prom. My Aunt Sealy fixed my hair up in curls. Aunt Sealy is my father's younger sister. I didn't get to see her often, but she was a professional hair stylist and was kind enough to style my hair.

On the day of the prom, I didn't see or hear from Lamont. About an hour before we were supposed to leave, he showed up and told my mother he couldn't take me. He made a lame excuse about not having the right shirt to wear. Once I heard the news, I was determined that I was not going. My mother told me I should go by myself. After all, she'd spent $80 on my dress, and my aunt had done my hair. She was not going to let me miss this night. I didn't want to go by myself, but I listened to my mother, and her friend drove me to the dance.

When we arrived, I saw couples going in and everyone looked great. Some of the girls wore sequined dresses, while the guys were very handsome in their tuxedos. I felt awkward about walking in by myself, so my Aunt Tammy called over one of the girls I knew and asked if I could go in with her and her date. It was so embarrassing, but they said it would be okay if I walked in with them. It seemed like everyone had a date except me. I was so uncomfortable about being there alone.

Our prom was in the school cafeteria, but the decorations changed everything. You wouldn't think this was the same room where we ate lunch every day. There were flowers everywhere and white lights hung on the walls. The tables had burgundy and gray tablecloths—our class colors. I sat at a corner table and watched everyone smiling, dancing, and having a good time. A few people came over to talk to me, but I felt out of place because I was there by myself. I picked up a plate of food, which I barely ate, had my picture taken, then called my mother and told her I wanted to come home. Instead of having her friend come back to get me, she sent my brother and his friends to the school, and they walked me home. It was awkward walking through the streets in my prom dress beside my brother and his friends, who were dirty from playing football. I found out the real reason Lamont canceled on me a few days later. He made plans with someone else, a woman closer to his age. I guess he thought, why go to a junior prom with a 16-year-old when he could go out with a sure thing.

Right before his high school graduation, Marcus told me he would be going into the Air Force. I was proud of him, but I was going to miss him like crazy. He was leaving toward the end of the summer, so I spent as much time with him as I could.

One day, I went to see him, and two of his friends showed up.

A little while later, two girls showed up as well. I think one of the girls liked Marcus, and they weren't pleased to see me. I felt very uncomfortable, so I decided to leave.

While walking down the street, I heard Marcus yelling, "Run!" I turned around to see the girls following me. Instead of running, I stopped and waited for them. Once they reached me, one of the girls started swinging on me. I fought back as best I could before Marcus broke up the fight. I found out later that one of Marcus' friends put the girls up to fighting me. They did it as a dare. Marcus didn't like the idea of them coming after me. In that moment, he saw the girls as bullies, and he doesn't like bullies. I didn't run because I felt that would only make the situation worse, so I stopped. If there was going to be a fight, I was going to face it head-on. I haven't been in many fights in my life, but the few times it did happen, I never ran away. I remember being at Marcus' house when they were having people over to celebrate him going into the military. That was the first time I met his dad. I bought Marcus one of those giant cards they used to sell. On the inside of the card, I wrote a note expressing how much I cared about him and how much I was going to miss him. His father must have read the card because when I was introduced to him, he looked at Marcus, then back at me, and asked, "Do you love him?" I was so surprised by the question. All I could do was make this weird little sound that made everybody laugh.

We had been spending time together for about a year at this point, and our relationship was never defined. We never put a label on it, but I felt he cared about me. During the time we spent alone, there was a lot of kissing and touching, but he never pressured me to take things further. Then came the night we decided we would take that next step. I don't remember having any conversation about it; there just seemed to be a mutual agreement that it was time. I had only been with one person before Marcus, and I was nervous; I didn't want to disappoint him. He was very gentle with me, and we had an enjoyable experience.

I found out years later that it was his first time. If he felt any nervousness that night, he hid it very well. He had this way of looking at me with a smile that always made me feel good. He told me that he liked seeing my facial expressions during our intimate moments, and that's what made him smile. On the day he was leaving for basic training, his family allowed me to go with them to the airport to see him off. He had gone to the airport ahead of us and was surprised to see me. We hugged and promised to write to each other.

A month later, I started my senior year of high school. I developed an attachment to Marcus' grandmother, Miss Estelle. She was a sweet lady who was always nice to me. Even after Marcus was gone, I would stop by their house on my way to school to say hello. I would walk up onto the porch, ring the bell, and watch her walk toward me through the screen door. There was a red and white metal glider sofa and two red metal chairs on the porch. I enjoyed sitting and chatting with her. From time to time, I would sit with her and watch television or listen to her talk about her experiences as a young woman. I came to regard her as a second grandmother.

Senior Year

My senior year of high school was pretty typical. Tammy and Marie were my core group of friends. We were looking forward to graduation. My two favorite teachers were my English teacher, Ms. Tonkins, and my math teacher, Mr. Wrobleski. Ms. Tonkins wasn't much older than us; I believe she was in her late 20s. In her class, we were reading *The Great Gatsby*, *Othello*, and *Macbeth*. Her class started me on my love of reading. I got into Harlequin romance novels and acquired quite a collection over the next few years.

I was never a great math student. All of those numbers and formulas are like Greek to me, but Mr. Wrobleski was always patient and took the time to make sure we understood how to get the answers. Math class was early in the morning, and Mr. Wrobleski would bring in a box of donuts to share with the class. The jelly-filled were my favorites, and at the end of class, if there were any left over, he would give them to me.

When it was time for my senior prom, Marcus was away in the Air Force. I ended up going with the brother of my friend Chantell, aka Shuggie. Shuggie was a couple of years older than me and had two small sons. I met her at school through my friend Lisa. Shuggie used to go to Shake n' Bake Skating rink every Friday night, and I went a few times, too. Her brother Carlo was in some of my classes, and I thought he was a nice guy. He seemed kind of quiet like me, and we always got along. Since neither of us had dates for the prom, we went together as friends.

Shuggie was very good at doing hair, and a lot of girls from the neighborhood paid her to style their hair. I asked my mom for money to buy a relaxer so I could get my hair done. I knew she received her weekly child support check from my father, so I was surprised when she said she didn't have any money. When I started to question her about it, I was cut short by the look on her face, like, "Don't you dare question me."

Shuggie washed and styled my hair for me anyway, but because it rained that day, the humidity turned my hair into a frizzy mess. I wore a long white dress with spaghetti straps, which was trimmed in black. I paired it with a bolero jacket. Carlo wore a white suit with a red bow tie and cummerbund. We made quite a pair. One of the girls in our class came to the prom wearing a tux instead of a gown, and it looked cute on her. It wasn't the sort of thing you'd expect to see, but on her it worked. She and her date made a very handsome couple. Everyone looked so grown-up: the girls in gowns, high heels, lipstick, and eye shadow, the guys in tuxedos and dress shoes. We were looking forward to graduation and our plans for the future. After prom, Carlo's mom picked us up and dropped me at home.

June 9, 1985, was graduation day. I turned 18 a month before and was making plans to leave home. I spent the last few years living a life of fear, anxiety, and frustration. I experienced abuse that no child should have to endure and had no idea if or when it could start up again. I watched my mother lose herself in addiction and an abusive relationship. I knew the only way to free myself from this hell was to remove myself from that household, and now that I was 18, no one could stop me. I talked to my grandmother about coming to live with her, and she agreed. When I walked down the aisle of the auditorium, I saw my mother, grandmother, and grandfather cheering and clapping. They set up seats for the senior class on the stage. Once the whole class was on stage and I went to sit down, my chair collapsed, and I almost hit the floor. One of my classmates caught me and helped me get into another chair.

I looked out into the crowd and spotted my father sitting in the back row. I was happy he was there since I hadn't seen him in a while. After the ceremony, he came over to congratulate me but didn't stay to celebrate with us. I wasn't surprised since he and my mother didn't get along. They could be in the same room and be cordial, but not for long. One of them always ended up leaving.

Two days after graduation, I moved out of my mother's house and into my grandmother's house. I didn't tell my mother I was leaving. Spending the weekend with my grandmother was normal, but this time, I wasn't coming back. I put everything I could carry into plastic bags and left. A couple of weeks later, she was evicted from her house and ended up coming to stay with my grandmother until she found a new place. When she left my grandmother's house, I didn't go with her. She was moving into her new place with Marvin, and I was not going back to that situation.

Coming of Age

I lived with my grandmother for about a year. I wasn't going to college because I wasn't sure what I wanted to do, I knew we couldn't afford it, and I didn't want to spend another four years in school. Knowing that I had to find something to do, I enrolled in a program to learn about computers and data processing. The program was only nine months long and included job placement opportunities at the end. After about three months, I got bored with the program and dropped out.

In the summer of 1986, my Aunt Tammy was moving into her own place, and I decided to go with her. Tammy is only five years older than I am, so she was more like a big sister than an aunt. It was fun living with Tammy because with her, I didn't have the rules I had when I lived with my grandmother. I didn't have any rules at all. My cousins and I could bring boys into the house and do pretty much anything we wanted.

Tammy's three children were young, and I helped out by babysitting anytime she wanted to go out. Her oldest son had cerebral palsy and needed special attention. He couldn't speak, walk, or do anything for himself. Taking care of him took a lot out of her, so

I pitched in to give her a break sometimes.

Her next-door neighbor's three sons were around my age. One weekend, their cousin Devon from Virginia came to visit. He was easy on the eyes, and I was very attracted to him. He was about my height, maybe an inch or two taller than my five feet five inches. His hair was brown and cut very short. He had mocha brown skin and a very toned body. Devon was visiting for the weekend before leaving for basic training in the Army Reserves. After spending a day and a half talking and hanging out with him, I did something very unusual for me. I decided to have sex with him. In the past, I would wait for months before taking that step with a guy.

There weren't many guys before Devon. At the time that we met, I was getting over losing Marcus. He met a girl while he was away in the service, and they got married. I was completely caught off guard because I didn't know he was seeing anyone. I don't know why I thought that. He was handsome, smart, and a nice guy. I'm sure there were plenty of girls who liked him. We were never officially a couple, but I didn't think about the possibility of him getting serious about anyone else.

I cared for him very much and was hoping that as time went on, our relationship could develop into us becoming an official couple and maybe more. It broke my heart when I heard the news. I remember thinking, *You're 19 years old, how are you getting married? What about me? Why wasn't I the one?* But what could I do? I wanted him to be happy. I had no choice but to accept his decision.

Being with Devon was a way to take my mind off Marcus. We spent a very nice night together, then he left. I didn't expect to hear from him, but he did write me a letter after a few weeks.

About two months after Devon left, I found out I was pregnant. I thought to myself, *"Oh my God, what am I going to do?"* A part of me was excited about having a baby. Another part was scared to death. I was 19 years old with a high school education and no job or a place of my own. My next thought was, *How is Devon going to react?* I was pretty sure it was not in his plans to have a baby with a girl he barely knew. I wrote him a letter and told him I was pregnant. I was anxious about his reaction, but he had to be told.

I called my mother to tell her about the baby. I was a little nervous about how she might take the news. The conversation went something like, "Hey, how are you? Are you working today?"

She said, "I'm off work today."

Then I said, "Good, I'm pregnant."

She kinda chuckled a little and said, "Okay, that's nice." I think she was happy about becoming a grandmother. She liked telling that story. She thought the way I blurted out the news was funny.

I was especially worried about telling my father. I hadn't spoken to him much since my high school graduation. Although we weren't close, I was still worried about his reaction. I didn't want to disappoint him or my mother by getting pregnant so young and not having a way to take care of myself or a child.

I remember telling him I was going to have a baby. He said, "Hold on a minute." He put the phone down, and I could hear him in the background telling his girlfriend he was going to be a grandfather. He sounded excited about it. Neither of my parents asked a lot of questions. My mother asked who the father was, and I explained he was someone who wasn't around anymore. They didn't press the issue; they just accepted the fact that this was happening.

About a week after I sent the letter to Devon, I got a phone call, and as I expected, he was less than thrilled. The first question I got was, "Is it mine?"

Well, I had to think about that because I did spend time with someone else after Devon left. When the doctor told me how far along I was, I pulled out my calendar and started counting the weeks back, which led me to the weekend I spent with Devon.

He wasn't hearing it and wanted me to consider terminating the pregnancy. That was never something I wanted to do. I needed to reconcile in my mind that I was going to be raising this baby on my own. When he came home after basic training, we talked. He asked me again about having an abortion. I told him I was not doing that. I understood that he had doubts about being the father since we didn't know each other that well. I suggested taking a blood test after the baby was born so he would know for sure. He made it pretty clear that he didn't want anything to do with the situation, and he went back home to Virginia. I didn't see or hear from Devon again until after the baby was born.

Preparing to be a single mom was scary. I wasn't working and didn't know how I was going to take care of myself and a baby. Living with Aunt Tammy was easy. She provided a place to sleep and food to eat. All I did was babysit once in a while. Thankfully, she let me continue to stay with her while I was pregnant. Her leasing office found out I was staying with her and said I had to leave since I wasn't on the lease. She asked if I could stay until after I had the baby, and they told her no. She took a big risk and allowed me to stay anyway. I will be forever grateful to my Aunt Tammy for that. She also helped me apply for public assistance, and I got medical assistance, food stamps, and a monthly check.

The experience of being pregnant took some getting used to. The first time I felt the baby move was weird and amazing. Knowing there was an actual person growing inside my body was overwhelming. This little person was depending on me for his very existence, and I wanted to do everything I could to protect him. Some nights it was hard to get comfortable because he kept moving around. He was very active in the womb. I sat up at times and watched my stomach move up and down as he kicked. As he was growing and I was getting bigger, whenever I rubbed my belly and felt him move, it was as if he was responding to my touch. That brought a sense of peace that let me know we would be okay.

The morning of May 31, 1987 (about a week and a half past my due date), I got up and went into the bathroom. I noticed that I was spotting and got nervous that something might be wrong. Having birthed three babies herself, my Aunt Tammy thought it might be the beginning of labor. She called my grandmother, and they took me to the hospital. It turns out she was right, but the doctor said it was too soon for me to be admitted. They sent me home and told me to come back once the contractions started. At that point, I wasn't feeling any pain. My grandmother thought I should keep moving in order to induce labor, so they made me go outside and walk around the block. All of this was happening on a Sunday morning. On the Friday before, I was in the hospital where the doctors gave me medicine to induce labor because I was past my due date. I was supposed to go back on Monday so they could try again. I guess the medicine from Friday took a couple of days to kick in.

Later that afternoon, I started feeling pain every few minutes. I called my mom and dad, and my mother met us at the hospital. The doctor confirmed I was definitely in labor, and I was admitted. I wasn't dilating fast enough, so they made me walk along what seemed like a mile-long hallway. It was annoying for me to pass the waiting room and see my family members sitting and watching television while I was doing all this walking by myself trying to get this baby ready to make his appearance.

The time finally came when I could lie down and try to relax in between contractions. When they took me into the delivery room, I was so nervous.

I said to my mother, "Why did I do this?"

She smiled, saying, "It's too late for that now. It'll be okay, you've got this."

I remember there was a mirror in the delivery room where you could watch your child being born. My mother kept trying to get me to look in the mirror and see the baby coming out. The pain was so bad that all I wanted to do was get the baby out. I thought it was bad enough that I had to feel the pain; I didn't want to see it, too. I was pushing for what felt like forever.

At one point, the doctor said, "Okay, Chanel, I see the head. We're almost there."

Then all of a sudden, he couldn't see the head anymore. This happened two or three times before I gave one final push and felt the baby slip out of my body. Once he was out and I heard him cry, I felt a great sense of relief. I thought the hard part was over.

The nurse cleaned him up and brought him to me. I looked at his little face and felt a joy I had never felt before. My mom asked if I wanted to hold him for a while, but I was so tired, all I wanted to do was sleep. I held him for a few minutes before the nurse took him to the nursery. I named my little boy Brian after my brother. We were close growing up, and I liked the sound of the name.

I woke up in the recovery room surrounded by my mother, grandmother, and my brother.

He looked at me with a smile and said, "That's one funny-looking baby you've got there."

I playfully slapped him on the arm, and everyone laughed.

My grandmother said, "No, he's not. He's a beautiful little pink baby." For a long time, she called him Pinky because his skin was light. After about two days in the hospital, I took Brian home.

Life as a new mother was an adventure. Late-night feedings, sterilizing bottles, diaper changes, and worrying about what I might be doing wrong, it was nerve-wracking. I remember coming downstairs with Brian, and he was only wearing a diaper. My grandmother said he should be wearing a t-shirt, but I thought he was okay because it was a warm day, and I didn't want him to get too hot. She insisted that I put a t-shirt on him. I figured she raised five children, so she knew best, and as a new mom, there was a lot I could learn from her. My mom came to visit, and she and my grandmother took Brian out for a walk in his stroller. Mama said I couldn't go out because I was still recovering. I felt fine, but apparently, a new mom needed to stay inside for the first few weeks after having a baby.

My mother was excited about being a grandmother and decided to go into a program to get off drugs. She wanted to be around to watch her grandson grow up. I was happy that she wanted to get sober and hoped that we could rebuild our relationship.

A month after Brian was born, I reached out to Ms. Estelle because I wanted her to meet him. When I spoke with her, I found out Marcus was home on leave. I hadn't communicated with him since I let him know I was pregnant. After he got married, we wrote a couple of letters to each other. Once I wrote to him that I was pregnant, the communication fell off. I guess at that point, there was an unspoken decision that we would move on with our separate lives. He was stationed in Germany, and in my mind, he was living his life and being a husband. A part of me was excited about the thought of seeing him again, but the other part was nervous about meeting his wife. I hoped he was happy, but I missed my friend.

His grandmother and I set a date and time for me to come over. When I got to the house, he wasn't there. It was good to see Ms. Estelle, and she thought Brian was so cute.

Walking into their house, I'd go past the living room, down a short hallway, and into the dining room, which was right next to the kitchen. Beside the dining room table was a La-Z-Boy recliner, and in the corner was a TV set. I sat on the recliner with Brian lying across my lap while Ms. Estelle sat on a chair next to me. As we chatted, I heard the front door open and close, then Marcus walked into the room. He looked as handsome as always, and I couldn't help but smile as he walked over to see the baby.

As it turned out, his wife didn't come home with him. I found out later that things weren't working out, and they were separating. Marcus was home for two weeks, and he came to Aunt Tammy's to spend time with me and Brian. He was a little angry when I told him Brian's dad was no longer in the picture. He thought it was messed up that Devon had walked out on his responsibilities as a father. He let me know that if I needed anything, all I needed to do was ask. After he went back to Germany, we kept in touch through letters.

When Brian was four months old, it was time to move out on

my own. I found a two-bedroom apartment that was subsidized, and I could afford the rent with the monthly check I was getting. My brother moved in with me to help with expenses. The building sat on Woodland Avenue in West Baltimore, right off Reisterstown Road.

The neighborhood wasn't the best, but it was a start. Directly across the street from my building was a big, boarded-up house surrounded by bushes and grass that desperately needed cutting. It looked like one of those houses in the movies that scare all the neighborhood kids.

I moved into my first apartment with a sofa and chair that I bought from a thrift store. I had a full-size box spring and mattress, a chest of drawers, a small TV set, and a bassinet for Brian. It wasn't much, but it was mine.

Having my own place was liberating—a space just for me and my little boy. I made my own rules and had no one to answer to. I still wasn't working, so my days consisted of taking care of the baby, watching PBS cartoons with him in the morning, and soap operas in the afternoon. Some days, I put him in his stroller, and we'd take the long walk to my grandmother's house or take the bus to Tammy's house.

One day, I put Brian in the bassinet while I went into the bathroom. When I came back to the bedroom, he was lying on the bed watching television. I was so surprised. I remember thinking, *How did you get there? That's not where I left you!* Brian could barely sit up on his own, but somehow, he lifted himself up on the side of the bassinet and tumbled onto the bed. It's a good thing I put the bassinet next to the bed, otherwise, my baby would have fallen onto the floor. Thankfully, he was okay.

Marcus is Back

I had settled into my apartment when Marcus returned from Germany and was stationed at a base in Maine. He came home on leave, and I invited him over to see my new place. I missed him so much and was excited to see him again. He walked from room to room, checking the place out. The apartment consisted of one large living/dining room area, a small kitchen (just enough room for one person), my room that I shared with my baby, my brother's room, and a small bathroom. He said the place looked nice, then gave me a big hug that seemed to last forever. Marcus always gave the best hugs.

We sat and talked for a while and watched TV, then he spent the night. Whenever he was home on leave, we would spend time together. After about a year, he was discharged from the Air Force. Once he was home full-time, I thought our relationship would progress and we would spend more time together, but that's not what happened. He moved back home with his mom and grandparents and started a new job. He was newly single and taking advantage of his new status. Marcus spent some of his weekends on the Eastern Shore, where he had family. While he was spending time with family, he was also hitting the clubs, drinking, and hanging out with other girls.

Despite the time we spent together and my growing feelings for him, Marcus and I were never in a committed relationship. We never went out together, we only spent time in my apartment. Although I wanted a defined and committed relationship with him, I never told him. I just looked forward to whatever time he made for me. I was never one for confrontation, and I wasn't very good at verbal communication. I was always afraid of offending people and of rejection. Sometimes two or three weeks would pass when I wouldn't see Marcus at all, but any time he called and wanted to come over, I never turned him down. I was always available.

Looking back on it now, I shouldn't have been so available. Why would he do anything different if I didn't give him a reason to change?

A few months after Brian's second birthday, I found out I was pregnant again. I was happy to be having a baby with Marcus and hoped this would bring about a positive change in our relationship. But again, I would be disappointed.

When I told him the news, he wasn't exactly thrilled. The first thing he said was, "I'm not ready to be a father."

I don't know why I expected a different reaction. We weren't spending a lot of time together, and although I felt he cared about me, I wasn't sure what his actual feelings were when it came to me. We talked about the possibility of not having the baby. I considered that he didn't feel he was ready. I also thought if I had the baby, I might be left to care for two children on my own, and I was having a hard enough time with one.

When we talked again, I agreed to terminate the pregnancy. I made the appointment and hoped that he would go with me for support. I ended up going alone while Marcus went to work. The process was set up in two appointments. The first was for an examination and counseling. The second was for the procedure itself. I went for the preliminary appointment, and while I was waiting in the exam room, I kept thinking about what I was about to do and why I was doing it. Terminating my pregnancy was not something I wanted to do. I was only doing it because of Marcus; it was what he wanted.

I couldn't go through with it, and when the doctor came in, I told him I changed my mind. I couldn't face Marcus to tell him in person about my decision. I wrote a letter letting him know I was going to have the baby. Just like with my first pregnancy, I had to accept I would be doing this on my own. It was about five months before we spoke again.

I found out years later that there were conversations between my family and his behind the scenes. I was told my mother and grandmother said some things to Marcus' mother that led her to believe he was willing to put me in a dangerous situation to get out of being a father. My family members led them to believe terminating the pregnancy could put my life at risk, and Marcus wanted me to have the procedure anyway. None of this was true, but the conversations caused a great deal of anger and hurt feelings. Ms. Estelle stopped talking to me because she thought I took part in creating that narrative. After all, I was the one who gave my family their phone number. I gave their number to my mother and grandmother because they wanted to talk with Marcus about taking responsibility for our child. I regret that I wasn't strong enough to ask them to stay out of it. Marcus and I were both adults, and I should have dealt with him myself. It hurt me to lose my connection with Ms. Estelle because we had become very close.

When I was six months pregnant, Marcus called to check on me. I was surprised and happy to hear from him. He started checking in regularly over the next few weeks, then he came to see me. When he came to see me, we didn't talk about why he stayed away. We just picked up where we left off: hanging out, watching TV, and spending the night. I was so happy he was coming around that I didn't press the issue. I never wanted to rock the boat because I felt I would push him away. I realize now that I never had him, at least not the way I wanted him.

I remember one particular night when Marcus came to see me. I was standing at the window looking out at the neighborhood when he walked up behind me and put his arms around my waist to rest his hands on my belly. He leaned down, kissed my cheek, and told me he loved me. That was the first time he said those words to me, and I felt butterflies in my stomach. I lay my head back against his chest, put my hands on top of his, and said, "I love you too." I thought maybe we could make something work. He would be there for me and our child, and he would be a father figure for Brian as well. That good feeling lasted for a while, then the visits became sporadic again.

On the morning of January 14, 1991, I started having pain in my lower abdomen and my back. I called Marcus to let him know I was going to the hospital. He had already left for work, and he didn't have a cell phone back then, so I wasn't able to reach him. My mom and my Uncle Irvin took me to the hospital and stayed with me while I was in labor. A little past noon, they went out to get food. The doctor assured them it would be hours before the baby came. The baby had other ideas. By the time my mom and uncle got back to the hospital, my second baby boy had entered the world. I named him Kevin.

A few hours later, I called to share the news with Marcus that his first son was born. He wasn't at home, so I spoke with his mom. I told her I had a baby boy and was surprised when she responded, "I know, I was called and told." From the tone in her voice, I got the feeling that she was not happy that the news had not come from me.

I called and spoke with Mama, who confirmed that she called Marcus' mom about the baby. I asked her why she did that, and she said, "We just wanted to let them know that the baby is going to need some things." I told her I should be the one to make that call. It bothered me because I felt they took that moment from me. I didn't get a chance to share with his father about Kevin's birth, and again, my family stepped into a situation that was my business. They treated me like a teenage mother, but I was 23 years old and a mother of two. My relationship with Marcus was already on shaky ground, and they made matters worse.

I didn't hear from Marcus until the day after I got home from the hospital. When he came to my apartment to see Kevin for the first time, my mom and brother were sitting in the living room. Without saying a word, Marcus walked by them and went straight to the bedroom. He looked into the bassinet at our sleeping baby boy and jokingly said, "He can't be mine; his head is too big." He didn't stay with us very long and seemed a little distant with Kevin. He didn't want to hold him, he just kept looking at him. After about an hour, he left and didn't come around very often.

Becoming a mom of two didn't feel as challenging as I expected. I was still receiving state assistance, and I'd notified the Department of Social Services about my second baby. I provided the necessary documentation, and they increased my benefits.

Dreams and Reality

When Kevin was born, Brian was three years old and wanted to be a good big brother. He was always trying to help me take care of the baby. He'd bring me pampers and wipes when it was time to change Kevin's diaper and try to help with feeding. He wanted to hold Kevin and give him his bottle. I made sure to spend one-on-one time with Brian so he didn't feel left out. I would read to him, and we would watch PBS Kids shows together.

The most challenging part of having two young children was traveling. Brian was in pre-school, and I took two buses to get him there every day. It was much easier bringing one child on the bus than two.

The process started the night before. I bathed both boys and decided what they were going to wear. I packed enough diapers and bottles for Kevin and threw in an extra outfit just in case. In the morning, I dressed both boys before getting myself ready. Our apartment was on the second floor, and I carried Kevin's stroller down the steps. When we walked to the bus stop, I had Brian hold onto one side of the stroller while I pushed it down the street. Once I saw the bus coming, I took Kevin out and folded the stroller because the aisle on the bus was too narrow to leave it open with the baby sitting in it.

I tried to sit as close to the front of the bus as possible. Between the diaper bag, the stroller, and finding seats for the three of us and all of their stuff, it could be a bit much, but we made it. Because Brian was only in school for half a day, I was happy they had a room where parents could stay while the kids were in the classroom. When I was pregnant with Kevin, I helped out at lunchtime, which allowed me to see how Brian interacted with the other kids.

A few weeks after I brought Kevin home from the hospital, I noticed that his left eye wasn't opening all the way. I took him to the doctor, and after examining him, they told me that he had ptosis of the left eye. This condition is also called *lazy eye,* which basically means the muscle in his eyelid was weak, causing it to sag. He needed surgery to fix it. I was extremely anxious about my baby having surgery, but if they didn't fix the problem and his condition worsened, he could have lost vision in that eye.

Marcus and I weren't on the best of terms, but I did let him know about the surgery. My grandmother went to the hospital with me on the day of Kevin's surgery. When I gave my baby to the nurse who was taking him into the operating room, I was scared that something would go wrong. Seeing how bothered I was, my grandmother suggested we get something to eat. She wanted to get me out of the hospital. She tried to keep me occupied, thinking it might help me not worry so much. Thankfully, the surgery went well, and I was able to bring him home the same day.

As Kevin grew, his doctor noticed he wasn't hitting certain milestones. Most children start saying words and phrases around the age of two and three. Kevin could say *Mama*, he could say *yes* and *no*, but he struggled putting together short phrases and sentences. If he wanted something like juice or a cookie, he couldn't verbalize it. He would take your hand, pull you over to the item he wanted, and point to it.

I had him evaluated at the Kennedy Kreiger Institute, and Kevin was diagnosed with developmental delays and difficulty with processing language. He was enrolled at the Gateway School, where he received speech therapy. He attended Gateway between the ages of three and nine.

I loved Gateway. The class sizes were small enough for the teachers to give individual attention to students who needed extra help. The teachers and staff were very patient, and their observation room let parents see what was happening in the classroom. I was relieved to know I could watch the interaction between the teachers and the children. Kevin seemed comfortable with the teachers and the other students. He's been able to continue his friendships with some of the kids he met at Gateway into adulthood.

When I became a mom, I decided to be a different type of

parent than what I saw growing up, especially when it came to discipline. In my family, spanking was the norm. I didn't want to be a spanking parent, but one day my little Brian put me to the test. He was about three years old. I can't remember exactly what he did, but my first reaction was to smack him on the butt. When I went to spank him, he ran from me. As I was chasing him around my living/dining room, he started yelling, "No, Mommy, please don't hit me!"

He ran under the dining room table and kept yelling the same words. I was so shocked by his reaction that I stopped and burst into laughter. A stranger witnessing this scene might have thought he was an abused child. I was so busy laughing, I couldn't spank him. All I could do was pull him out from under the table and hug him. Whatever it was he did, he got away with it that day.

Although I'm not a big fan of spanking, there were times my kids would get a smack on the hand for touching something they shouldn't or a pat on the butt if I had to correct them about something more than once. It didn't happen very often since, for the most part, my boys were good kids who did what they were told.

In the midst of taking care of the boys, I was still seeing Marcus. The relationship was pretty much off and on. There would be periods when we were good, seeing each other at least once a week, sometimes more. I enjoyed our time together, but I wished he would interact more with the boys. Most of the time, when he came over, it was after their bedtime.

One time, Marcus took Kevin to his dad's house. Marcus's

older sister Joann was visiting from out of town, and he wanted Kevin to meet her. When they came back, Marcus told me how Joann got Kevin to walk to her. He was just starting to take a few steps here and there, and that was the first time Marcus saw him walk. I was happy he took that time to spend with his son.

One evening, Marcus came by to hang out with me. My cousin Dana was staying with me at the time. Marcus and I were going to see a movie, our first time going out instead of just watching television and going to bed. I was excited to go on an actual date. When Dana heard what we were doing, she chimed in and said, "I wanna go."

Thinking about it now, I should have said no.

We agreed that she could come and off we went. When we got to the theater, Marcus went to buy our tickets and asked Dana for money for her ticket. "I don't have any money," was her response. Marcus was instantly annoyed.

We didn't see a movie that night. We ended up having a very awkward ride back to my apartment, where we watched television as usual. Marcus said that if Dana had told him ahead of time that she couldn't pay for her ticket, he would've paid for her. In his mind, she assumed he would pay for her even though she had invited herself. Looking back, it should have been made clear before we left the house, then he wouldn't have gotten mad. That was the one and only time he asked me to go out. I saw that as a missed opportunity to broaden the parameters of our relationship. Instead, things just went back to business as usual.

During my time with Marcus, I often questioned if he truly cared about me. In his presence, I felt peaceful and content. When I wasn't with him, I tried not to think about the possibility of him being with someone else.

We never talked about anything serious, partly because I didn't know how to have those conversations. I hadn't been serious about anyone before Marcus, so there was no need to talk about goals or dreams, the kind of talks committed couples have. When I think about it now, if he had asked those types of questions, I don't know how I would have answered since I didn't have any real goals or dreams. My only focus was doing what was needed to take care of my boys. Marcus would make statements like, "I love you to death, in my own way." I never really understood what "in my own way" meant, but I also never asked him to explain. I was just happy to hear him say he loved me.

I always felt that if you want a good relationship, you should treat people the way you want to be treated. It took a lot of years to realize that strategy doesn't always work. I would do little things for Marcus like sending *"Thinking of You"* cards, giving him back massages, and once I even made him dinner. He showed up late and didn't stay very long.

I had this fantasy about the life I wanted, living with Marcus and the two of us raising the boys together. I didn't think very far beyond that. I felt love for Marcus, but if anyone asked me what I loved about him, I'd be hard pressed to come up with a good answer. He would

71

only see me at night; we didn't go out in public together. I hadn't been introduced to anyone in his family outside of his mom and grandparents. Looking back on it, what I could say is that I enjoyed the way I felt when I was with him. I was comfortable in his presence. I felt happy lying next to him and safe with his arms around me. Once he was gone and days went by with no communication, I wondered if someone else was holding his attention.

Although he was helping to take care of Kevin financially, he never developed a father-son bond with him and that bothered me. He played with the boys whenever he came over before their bedtime, but it wasn't what I thought they needed. Other than the one time he took Kevin to his dad's house as a baby, Marcus didn't spend one-on-one time with him. It got to the point where I started to wonder what I was holding on to. I used to wonder if he kept coming around because he knew I'd always be there. I never said no when he wanted to come over. It seemed like everything was happening on his terms. I guess it was, because I allowed it to be that way.

I wish I were brave enough to have the conversation with Marcus that needed to be had. Because I was scared of hearing things I didn't want to hear, I did what I always did; I kept my feelings to myself.

After spending a pleasant night with Marcus, I received a letter that changed everything. The letter came from someone who claimed to have met me on the street. I didn't recognize the name on the return address, a P.O. box in Jessup. There is a state prison in

Jessup, Maryland. I surmised from the ID number after the name and the P.O. box address that the letter came from an inmate. The style of the address was similar to the letters I used to get from Uncle Ray when he was in prison.

In this letter, the writer described meeting me outside a laundromat on the corner of Park Heights and Woodland Avenue. He claimed he was driving a white BMW, as if that would impress me. I guess it would impress some people, but I've never been into material things like that. However, the fact that he knew about the laundromat where I went on Saturdays to wash my clothes told me he was familiar with the area.

I never paid much attention to guys who approached me on the street—not that it happened often. Even though I didn't know this person, or why anyone would write to me from jail. I was curious. I told Marcus about the letter and showed it to him. After reading the letter, he said, nonchalantly, "Hmm, impressive." Then he left.

Marcus's blasé attitude about the letter made me feel as if it didn't matter to him that another man was showing an interest in me. Did he think I wouldn't go anywhere? Did he believe that because I cared so much for him that I would continue to accept the little scraps of time he was willing to give me? At that moment, I realized the relationship I wanted, the dream of the four of us being a family, was not going to happen. I was tired of waiting for him. It was time to let go.

That was the last night we spent together. There was no conversation about it, no official ending to the relationship. We just didn't come together in that way anymore.

I've learned so much in the years since then. Now, I realize that I was asking for things neither of us was ready for. I wanted the fantasy of raising my sons in the same household with a man that I loved. I wanted to give them the family life I didn't have. The person I was back then was not good at communication. Both Marcus and I experienced traumatic situations that we had not dealt with properly.

We've shared several conversations over the past few years and concluded we had lots of growing to do. We weren't who we needed to be to have that life. Times have changed. Marcus and I can have mature conversations, and we have a friendship that is priceless to me. For that, I'm grateful.

Mom and Me

The relationship between a mother and daughter can be extremely close. A girl should be able to look at her mom as an example of things to do or how to be in life. My mother served as an example of what not to do, although in some cases, I made a lot of the same mistakes. My relationship with my mother had a lot of ups and downs. I loved my mother very much, but there were times when I did not like her.

A year after I moved in with my grandmother, she finally got away from Marvin. In my twenties, there was a period when I avoided being around her because I couldn't stand watching her hurt herself with her addiction, and I still held some resentment toward her because of what happened when I was a child. As I got older, I started to understand some of the decisions she made. At one point, she went into a rehab program and got off drugs. While celebrating the first anniversary of what would be her first attempt at sobriety, she spoke at a Narcotics Anonymous meeting about her abusive relationship and its effect on her life. She shared that she started using drugs as a way to be close to this man that she loved, since he was also an addict.

Despite her reasons for starting down this road to addiction, he constantly criticized her for using drugs. Her self-esteem was in the toilet. She stated that as much as she hated the way he treated her, "the worst thing of all was that he touched my child." I was not expecting her to bring up this subject. She and I never spoke about what happened to me, and here she was talking about it to a room full of strangers. She explained she took him back after the trial because he made threats toward her and her family. Given the control he had over her, I think she felt she had no choice. He broke her spirit with his physical and verbal abuse. It was embarrassing for me, but I think I understand why she did it. She may have felt some sense of guilt for not protecting me, and this may have been her way of apologizing. Sitting in this room full of strangers and listening to her talk about my trauma was very awkward. I kept my eyes on her, not wanting to make eye contact with anyone else. Hearing her speech and watching how she loved and cared for my children reminded me of how she was when my brothers and I were small. Over the years, she relapsed a couple of times before finally quitting for good. There came a time when I decided to let go of the hurt and resentment so that we could rebuild our relationship. Even after I forgave her, we never had that conversation.

In the last ten years of my mother's life, we were as close as a mother and daughter could be. We talked on the phone two to three times a day about any and everything. We spent almost every Saturday at Walmart and would take the kids to eat at Old Country

Buffet. We liked going there because Kevin was a very picky eater, and thanks to the variety of options, he could always find something he would eat at the buffet.

It felt so good when my mother found someone who made her truly happy. She met a lovely man named Sam who treated her very well. He didn't judge her for her past and was there for her when she needed him. She started to struggle with her health, and he stood by her through it all. In February 2004, we gathered at my brother's house when my mother and Sam were married.

Unspoken Words

They say a little girl's first love is her father, a daddy who's there to make her feel loved and protected. He teaches her what the love of a man should feel like and shows her how she should be treated by the way he treats her mother.

I didn't experience the love of my father in a way that made me feel safe or protected. My father was absent from my life for most of my childhood. Except for some holidays or the occasional school shopping trip, we didn't see or hear from him.

One of my earliest memories of my father was when he picked up my brother Brian and me and took us to visit our grandmother at her house on Derby Manor Drive. The steps going up to her house felt like walking up a very steep hill. I remember her red and gray textured wallpaper that felt like velvet when I ran my hand over it. I had never seen wallpaper like that in any other house. Nana, as we called her, made us creamed chipped beef on white toast. Since we only saw her a few times a year, I feel like I never got to know her.

On the occasional Saturday, we would go to my dad's apartment to spend the day with him and his girlfriend, Lucille. Sometimes he took us out for dinner, and other times he made dinner for us at home. When we asked to spend the night, he always said no. It was disappointing. The reason was always the same; he didn't have room for us since there was only one bedroom. We offered to sleep on the couch or even on the floor. The answer never changed. It seemed like he didn't want us around for more than a few hours.

After going through one of the worst experiences of my life, I needed him to save me from a terrible situation. He wasn't there for me. He left me to live in a house where he knew I was being abused. It took a very long time for me to make peace with that and to forgive him. My only regret is that we never talked about it. I never asked how he could leave me to endure such an unspeakable experience. I'm not sure if there was any answer he could've given that would've made it okay. I decided to let go of the hurt and the anger because it served no purpose in my life. Holding on to those feelings wasn't going to hurt him as much as it did me.

I felt a glimmer of hope for building a relationship with my dad when I shared that he was going to be a grandfather. I was so nervous about his reaction to the news. Even though we weren't close, I didn't want to let my father down first by getting pregnant at 19, then by having to struggle as a single parent.
Shortly after getting the news, he started to check in with me to see how I was doing, and that made me feel he cared and that I mattered to him.

But after Brian was born and then Kevin, our relationship didn't grow the way I hoped it would. We talked only once in a while, and still didn't see each other very often. He would show up at Christmas with a bunch of presents for the boys, which were always appreciated, but it was still not what I needed from him as my dad. Just like when I was a child, I needed him to be more present in my life. I needed my dad to call more often. It would have been wonderful to have father-daughter time, getting together for lunch or dinner. I needed him to make me feel the love of a father, even though it would be years before I heard him say the words.

I never heard him talk about his father, so I can only assume that either the relationship wasn't good, or it was non-existent. Maybe he didn't know how to be the dad we needed. Maybe, he thought supporting us financially was good enough, but what we needed most was his time and attention. We needed consistency, love, and protection, and we didn't get that.

I've also wondered if part of the reason my father stayed away was because he was avoiding my mother. From what I understand, their relationship didn't end well. I hoped he wouldn't allow any bad feelings he may have had about her to affect his relationship with my brother and me.

When I told him my mother was sick and would probably pass soon, he let me know he would not be going to her funeral. That gave me pause. I felt he should have been there as emotional support for his children, who were losing their mom, despite his feelings toward her. I don't know if he still harbored anger toward her after so many years or if he never got over the way their relationship ended, but I wish he could have put those feelings aside and been there for us as our dad.

As I was getting older and having my own children, I wanted to make sure they always knew they were loved. When my dad got sick and his condition started to deteriorate, I began to wonder what I would say at his funeral. There were times when I didn't know what I would say about him as a person because I felt I didn't know him well. As I thought more about it, there were two specific memories I could highlight: when I was on the stage at my high school graduation and spotted him in the back of the auditorium, and when he taught me how to drive when I was 30 years old.

I'll never forget his driving lessons. I finally decided to learn how to drive because I didn't want to travel with four kids on the bus. I remember he picked me up in his sky-blue Chevy Malibu and took me to the parking lot of the Baltimore Polytechnic Institute, which we call Poly, and tried to show me how to parallel park. It took a lot of effort, but we finally got it. All these years later, when I'm driving, I hear his voice telling me to watch my heavy foot when I'm going too fast. When stopping at a red light behind another car, he'd always say to make sure I could see their tires on the ground. That way, I'd know I wasn't so close that I couldn't go around them if necessary.

In the final months of his life, we started to communicate more often. I was pleasantly surprised to hear him say, "I love you," to me. We were ending a conversation, and right before we hung up the phone, he told me he loved me. In my head, I knew that he loved me as his child but hearing him say it for the first time brought me a sense of peace and joy. I smiled. He started saying it at the end of every phone call, and I was still getting used to hearing it.

I drove to Virginia to see him a few weeks before he died, and I was shocked by how much weight he had lost because of cancer. I know when people go through that, weight loss is a big part of what happens to the body but seeing his small frame and remembering the solid and healthy man he was just a few years before was daunting. I visited him once more before he left us, and even though he barely knew I was there, I was happy to have that time with him. I hugged him, something we rarely did during my lifetime, and I kissed him goodbye. I think that was a fitting way to end our chapter of life together. I am thankful for the memories that make me smile when I think of my dad.

Reclaiming My Voice

When I think about the Chanel I was as a little girl, a teenager, and a young woman, I think about the woman I am now, and what I might say to young Chanel. As a little girl, I learned to be quiet and to stay out of the way. As a teen, I learned to push my feelings down because speaking up didn't improve bad situations. As a young woman, I continued to push my feelings down because I was always worried about chasing away the people who were important to me. What I didn't realize was that speaking up for myself was what I needed to do. The voice I needed back then was silenced, and it would take years to get it back.

If I'm completely honest with myself, there are still times when I hold back my voice. I don't always feel confident in my ability to do what I want to do. I still worry about hurting the feelings of people I care about or making them upset. It always bothered me if I thought anyone was upset with me. I'm better than I was, but I am still a work in progress.

Reflecting on the first half of my life, I realize how often I've shifted and moved on from situations that weren't good for me or simply didn't serve me anymore. I left my mother's house with no plan for what to do or how to support myself. I decided to leave a relationship that wasn't going in the direction I wanted. I left the comfort of being with my aunt to begin my journey as a young mother. These are just a few instances where I was faced with a choice. I looked at the situation for what it was and chose to either stay or move.

Sometimes moving on can be scary because you don't know what the outcome may be. I remember a line from a television show I used to watch. The character said, and I'm paraphrasing, "When you take chances in life, sometimes good things happen and sometimes bad things happen, but if you don't take a chance, nothing happens." I've had my share of good and bad things, and I'm learning to take more chances.

My journey through this life has been interesting, and I have many more stories to share. I've made choices as an adult that caused me to question who I am and what makes me the way I am. Why did I ignore red flags for the sake of being in a relationship? Why did I put myself in situations I knew weren't good for me? As I continue my journey, the answers become clear, and I look forward to sharing the insights I have discovered.

The Story Continues…

Chanel is working on her second book, which continues where this one ends. It tells the story of her marriage, finding her career, raising a growing family, the rocky path to her current success, and how she became the confident woman she is today. Her story is heartwarming and heartbreaking. Like so many women, she's overcome challenges to find her inner strength and personal compass. It's a story she hopes women will read, discuss, use to help themselves look for their inner strength and peace, and share with the younger generations who are still finding their way.

www.ingramcontent.com/pod-product-compliance
Lightning Source LLC
Chambersburg PA
CBHW031223120626
46545CB00003B/970